This book belongs to

_____

Copyright © 2021 Humor Heals Us. All rights reserved. No part of this book may be reproduced in any form without permission in writing from the publisher. Please send bulk order requests to Humorhealsus@gmail.com Printed and bound in the USA. humorhealsus.com 978-1-63731-185-1

Felix the Farting Feline

the Farting Feline

by Humor Heals Us

He never stopped all through the day
Which made his owners bitter.
Because everywhere that Felix went,
It smelled like **kitty** litter.

Felix was affectionate.
He loved to rub on legs,
But suddenly he'd fart so bad.
It smelled like rotten **eggs**.

Everyone agrees Felix farts a special one,
Especially when he's chasing mice.
It smells like stinky cheese.
But to them, it smells so **nice**.

Sometimes he climbs the curtains
Or sharpens his claws on the chair.
But suddenly Felix will fart,
And the smells **invade** the air.

Felix was taken to the vet
To have a **vaccination**.
So overpowering were his farts,
The vet went on vacation.

Percy the Parrot lived there too.
He would stomp his feet.
When Felix farted near his cage,
It turned up Percy's **heat**.

"Felix my friend I must say,
Your farts are **stinky** - poo!
Go and find another home!
I need some space from you."

One night an evil burglar
Broke into Felix's house.
He knew the human family was out
And tiptoed like a mouse.

Suddenly, Felix was there in a flash.
He jumped up on the bench.
The burglar just dropped everything
When he smelled the **horrid** stench.

Made in the USA
Las Vegas, NV
06 September 2021

29724082R00021